PRAYER BOOK OF THE ANXIOUS

JOSEPHINE YU

Prayer Book
of the Anxious

ELIXIR PRESS

PUBLISHED BY ELIXIR PRESS

P.O. Box 27029

Denver, Colorado 80227

www.elixirpress.com

Library of Congress Cataloging-in-Publication Data

Names: Yu, Josephine, author.

Title: Prayer book of the anxious / Josephine Yu .

Description: Denver, Colorado : Elixir Press, [2016]

Identifiers: LCCN 2015048259 | ISBN 9781932418583 (alk. paper)

Classification: LCC PS3625.U156 A6 2016 | DDC 811/.6--dc23

LC record available at http://lccn.loc.gov/2015048259

Cover art by Guy Laramée

Book design by Alban Fischer

10 9 8 7 6 5 4 3 2 1

FIRST EDITION

For Royal

MY DEAREST, MY MOST COMFORTABLE OF LOVES

Contents

Introduction

Josephine Yu's *Prayer Book of the Anxious* is part meditation, part myth-creation, part self-help manual, and all poetry. In finely wrought image and skillfully woven series-within-series, this collection explores the twistings and windings of a contemporary mind and soul in search of peace. The speakers of these poems configure and reconfigure their understandings of how an individual, in conflict with herself and her religious and cultural traditions, can make sense of emotional contortion and grief. These are essential, timely poems, and I could not put them down until I reached the final, satisfying line.

I confess that I opened the manuscript with a bit of trepidation. After all, who in the world is without anxiety? And who needs poems to add to that feeling? In fact, the book had hooked me already, with its tantalizing title. And I discovered that the poems not only exercise the language of fear but also exorcise that emotion through their interwoven fairy tales, fables, and myths (has there ever been a fairy tale that didn't generate dread?); prayers to saints; and personal lyrics that capture the complexities of familial and romantic relationships.

The fairytale and myth poems of the "Palm-Leaf Manuscript" poems make up one of the threads running through this intricately woven collection. The first of these prose poems, "A Myth from the Palm-Leaf Manuscript," tells two horrible stories of animal deaths, but the last paragraph points to the larger issues at stake for the entire book:

> This is the story the elders will tell when the wheat withers
> on the stalk and the firstborn swallow their tongues, the story
> they'll repeat when the cattle fall like trees and the trees fall
> like drunkards: this, the myth of the god of despair, who is
> the father of the god of attention.

I kept coming back to this poem, because it reveals so much about how to read this book—and about the nature of despair. It struck me as an elemental truth, expressed perfectly in the language of story, which is what the best myths do.

The second section, "Canticles, Maybe," introduces the prayers to various saints from the Roman Catholic tradition. Of these wonderful petitions, I would find it difficult to choose a favorite, though "Prayer to Saint Joseph: For the Restless" particularly stayed in my mind. Yu's easy humor (which appears even in some very grim situations!) launches this poem flawlessly—"Saint Joseph, stepfather of Christ, patron of moving, patron / against doubt, lead us not to Seattle or LA or SoHo / when unease thickens like lime calcifying / / in the porcelain basins of our chests." But this is not a joke, and the ending, still recalling the Pater Noster, offers an image both familiar and startlingly fresh:

> Still our hands as we pack. Remind us that the roughest fabric
> of the self will end up folded like a sweater
> in the suitcase, pilled and raveled and transcendent.

These are smart, savvy poems, but they are also humane in the best sense of that word: interested in the human and compassionate to all beings. Josephine Yu asks the right questions—"What animal am I?" and "Ready to go home?"—and the answers she gives are always those of an anxiety-born attention, not just to the self but to all of humanity. At the end of *Prayer Book of the Anxious*, our answer has to be yes, but in this ultimately outward-looking book, home is the world in which we all, nervously, exist.

Sarah Kennedy
Contest Judge,
The 15th Annual Elixir Press Poetry Award

I.

Apologia

The Compulsive Liar Apologizes to Her Therapist for Certain Fabrications and Omissions

Attic office, turquoise carpet, rock fountain
on the end table, its drowned gurgle—
I admit at first these filled me with contempt,
and the Madame Alexanders in the pram
made me uneasy. But I stayed out of pity
for your heart-embroidered vest
and your eagerness as you leaned toward me,
pen poised above a clipboard.

When you asked about my marriage, I lied. My job,
that too. When you asked for a dream, I confess
I gave my mother's, the one that woke her coughing,
thinking she'd choked on her sister's tangled, hip-length hair.
Truth is, I'm an only child.

But after you pulled the *Encyclopedia of Dreams*
from the shelf below the Hummels
and decoded the throat of hair as an estrangement,
spitting a little in your pleasure,
I invented others, presents I brought each Thursday at 11.
They fell from my lips as glossy and inevitable
as coupons from the Sunday paper,
and you translated them like fortunes in a dead language.

A gold bracelet in a well: an old friend will call.
A cut on my ring finger: desire for a lover.

A child crying on the doorstep of an empty house:
some unfinished task. Happiness: unspoken sorrow.

I wish I'd given you the real one, the only one
I dream each long, blank night:
my teeth crumbling, crown and cementum cracking.

I should have told you what I really wanted
when I woke at dawn, gasping—a gold tooth
to replace a molar, just one, anchored in my jaw,

slender threads of gold running deep to touch bone,
a gold tooth hidden in the back of my mouth
near the beginning of words, like a secret
or a blunt pain I could prod with my tongue,
a pain I could test and be sure of.

A Myth from the Palm-Leaf Manuscript

Remember the woman who told you she found a dead cat on her deck, fur matted with August rain, how her husband nudged it onto cardboard with his loafer and dropped it over the fence into the neighbor's azaleas? Make her you, you ten, her husband your father, before the divorce.

Make the cat a mole, small, the size of the hollow rock with the spare key. A star-nosed mole, *Condylura cristata*, who breathes underground, blind, whose snout tentacles sniff out and consume the grout and worm faster than the eye can follow.

Make August February, the shoe a shovel. Let the shovel crack the frozen fur. Say you turned your face and saw your father's shirts brittle on the clothesline, glazed with ice, and heard the shovel ring like the clapper of the church bell.

This is the story the elders will tell when the wheat withers on the stalk and the first-born swallow their tongues, the story they'll repeat when the cattle fall like trees and the trees fall like drunkards: this, the myth of the god of despair, who is the father of the god of attention.

A History of Home

WITH LINES FROM TACITUS

Long months they foraged in a wilderness
    of cardboard boxes,

       the empty bureaus and bookcases towering
where the movers set them,
        a knobbed and runged forest.

They slept on blankets, avoiding
    the stacked bones of the bed frame.

For dinner, they ate cereal from newspaper bowls,
      oven gravestone-cold,

as moths slipped between loose Jalouise panes
    and wove a cat's cradle around the bare bulb.

[Ethnographer's note: Because they didn't know better, they called it "civilization."]

•

The first financial report to the Ministry of Commerce and Longing
was succinct, scrawled on the back of the power bill.

"No economy
to speak of

Little to barter
but light bulbs
and toilet paper

Jasmine vines flare
across chain-link

But the soil
tamped by sun:

crusted, unfavorable
to fruit-bearing trees"

[Ethnographer's note: They wanted children to play in the cul-de-sac
of the hallway but the row of suburban bedrooms had been foreclosed.
This the gods refused them, whether in kindness or in anger I cannot say.]

•

Using flashcards, they memorized essential
phrases in the local dialect

>   *I'm sorry*
>   *move over*
>   *never again*
>   *in the spice drawer, behind the cumin*

until they were dreaming in the geography
of their adopted tongue:

>   verbs of boat-woven lakes,
>   prepositions of palm trees, conjunctions
> of Spanish moss and mosquitoes, and the most common

modifier, sometimes translated "sweltering,"
sometimes "humid"

[Ethnographer's note: When calling out to each other, they cupped their hands around their mouths, so their voices swelled to a fuller and deeper sound.]

•

They removed the doorknobs and soldered
the deadbolts, such was their commitment to stay.

Then, late summer labor—razing space
for crops of floor lamps and drying racks
heavy with hand-wash-only dresses—
followed by autumn expeditions to map the terrain

(which floorboards groaned at 2 a.m.
which cupboards could accommodate tall-necked
bottles of Belvedere vodka and olive oil,
under which window a book could be read
as the room filled with shadows).

Thus progress was made despite hardships.

At dusk, they listened for a stray cat's keening
and from the pitch
augured the coming week's weather:
F flat, more rain, and tomatoes soon furred with mold,
D major, a tornado to scatter the shingles
like religious tracts,
B sharp, a breeze to lift the veil of gnats.

[Ethnographer's note: All this is unauthenticated, and I shall leave it open.]

8

Why the Lepidopterist Lives Alone

Because he takes a first date to the butterfly conservatory,
and when the woman delights in white-hemmed wings
lighting on her ring finger, he corrects her:

"Mourning Cloaks exhibit territoriality by perching
on a high object. That one rests on your raised hand
should not be construed as intelligence or friendliness."

Because each antenna of the moth is a single filament
that tapers like his mother's fingers uprooting milkweed.

Because his bedroom is lined with maple display cases,
wings pinned to cotton batting like barrettes in a bride's hair.

Because he speculates that moths, being nearly blind,
are attracted to the hum of light bulbs, rather than the light,

and knows noctuid moths migrate using the moon
as a reference, adjusting their flight by 16 degrees
each hour to correct for the earth's rotation.

Because the most common butterfly is the Cabbage White
but he dreams of the Queen Alexandra's Birdwing,
found only in New Guinea. She lays her eggs
on the broad, poisoned leaves of pipe vines.

Because he tells a woman studying the Karner Blues
in the Museum of Comparative Zoology,
"Nabokov wrote *Lolita* on butterfly-hunting trips
across the western states. He distinguished species
by inspecting their genitalia under a microscope."

Because caterpillars release their skin in stages called *instars*.
To break through the old skin, they arch their backs
as if rising to a lover's stroke, as if bowed by orgasm.

The Fortune Teller Knows She'll Never Marry

Because she wakes one morning with hands
so swollen even her father's class ring
can't be worked over the stiff knuckle.
Because weevils writhe in her canister
of rice and the dough under the cheesecloth
veil refuses to rise and she draws three times
a worn Five of Cups from the tarot deck.

So when she traces a hopeful woman's
sloping heart line, she returns her folded bill
and foretells: "You give your love too easily,
you toss it like pennies into a well.
You'll come to know no more thrilling sound
than your own heart breaking like the crest
of a wave or the clapper of a glass bell."

Veneration of the Anxious

If grief is a motel where we each wait
alone in a room, listening
to the pillowcase seams unravel,

surely worry is a cathedral
where we congregate to practice
the sacred rites: the biting of nails
and the picking of the newest scab
or smallest ragged edge of skin.

Such holy ground and ancient customs.
Prayer of pacing, vestment of sweat,
the thumbing of buttons on tolerant cuffs.

We come to be consecrated
in dizziness, nausea, insomnia,
ecstatic to hear the chorus of heartbeats,
those hymns racing.

Autobiography of the Loneliest Man on Earth

I had a dog once, but I ran away.

     I have six brothers who each speak
a different language. I can say

        goodbye in Mandarin, Zulu, Russian,
Sanskrit, Greek, and Urdu.

I won the spelling bee in first grade and invited
        the word list to my birthday party.

I majored in the economics of frozen,
             single-serving pumpkin pie slices.

     I held a conch shell to my ear and heard
the hum of break room gossip. I knotted

        my bed sheets together to escape
from social obligations. I moved to a state with

        only one word for snow: impossible.
I bought a duplex across from a cemetery

and rented one side to mold. I walk
        the front lawn of graves before breakfast,

picking fists of carnations for my dining room table.

    After dinner I listen to telemarketers sing

        the legal hymns of cell phone contracts.

Still, I have a neighbor who's much lonelier.

        She married a split-rail fence.

Five minutes with her, and you *know* you know

nothing about fog escaping a meadow

        despite the embrace of cedar.

An Unfinished Fairytale
from the Palm-Leaf Manuscript

Once when Empathy and her younger sister, Longing, were my night nurses, Empathy tucked me in and began to tell me the story of a maiden who fell in love with her classmate, a fluttering, bird-boned girl with the chalky skin of the porcelain dolls the maiden unwrapped each Christmas but wasn't allowed to touch. The maiden skimmed the lake surface of the girl's hair with her fingertips and helped her write unsigned love letters to schoolboys. She memorized the girl's strange prayers and listened to her sigh over her crushes, stories the maiden pasted into her scrapbook like newspaper clippings of house fires.

In the fourth month, as the scrapbook billowed with smoke, a stranger called looking for "Elise"—a wrong number, yet each evening he called at dusk, his voice smearing like rain on a windshield until the maiden could hardly see. And each evening she answered *yes, yes,* and so learned to clip her vowels the way Elise had, learned the way Elise dusted the porridge with nutmeg, the way the lake had filled the vase of her chest with cold water and lilies. At dusk the maiden waited for the phone to ring, for wings to bloom from her shoulders, gift of a forgotten godmother...

Here Empathy dozed off before pinfeathers could prick the maiden's skin. I slipped from my bed, as children will do, and found Longing trying on my mother's lipstick. I asked if she'd ever been so in love she kept calling the same wrong number or so lonely she kept answering. She pressed her carnation lips together, pressed them against the full-length mirror on the bedroom door.

The Failed Revolutionaries Apologize to Their Foreign Sponsors

We admit we were disorganized, our numbers lower
than projected. The revised manifesto was lost
when the server crashed, and morale dropped after the third
shipment arrived with snout beetles rippling in the rice
and not one pack of Lucky Strikes—which is no excuse

for oversleeping on the morning of the coup, or leaving our nametags
swinging from lanyards in the mudroom, our sabers yawning
in their leather sheaths, our grandfathers' muskets locked
in leaden sleep in the curio case. The blades of our knives

snapped from their bone handles, clattering on the steps
of the capitol like a riot of macaws, though it hardly mattered,
what with the senators on recess, their secretaries out shopping
with state credit cards, charging silk scarves for the senators' wives,
silk chemises for their mistresses. No one heard

the echo of our boots scuffing the chert-veined marble
our grandfathers polished. We could have snapped
the spindly legs of Chippendale chairs for kindling
or torn down the drapes for jackets and bedrolls, honeyed
velvet the color of our wives' necks as they kneel at the river
to gather water in conch shells, lacking buckets.

When we left the curtains humming to their reflections,
we understood we'd become the failures our mothers predicted,

born as we were with the hangdog eyes of our fathers
and sloped foreheads of various estranged uncles.

However, I'd be lying if I said we aren't somewhat relieved
and looking forward to the familiar discomfort
of our pallets, the dream of the promised mattresses
with European pillow tops dissipating as we exhale
the usual ration of air, barely a cupped handful.

A Vindictive Son of a Bitch of a Poem

The woman sitting next to me in the theater
drove me insane texting on her cell phone with her acrylic nails:
click click click, ski chase down Mount Everest, *click click click*,
plot twist, *click click*, matching briefcase
exchange, *click click click*, the double agent *click click*
takes a bullet for his brother, the submarine *click click* operator.

You've heard me complain about cell phones before
and you might think this time I saw the woman's face lit up
in the blue glow and thought she looked like my sister
and then realized something about our common humanity.
Well, don't get your hopes up.

If you're expecting a moment of redemption
or a metaphor or anything other than the sound of my house key
squealing across the passenger door of her Jetta,
I'm sorry to disappoint you, but you've got the wrong poem.

This poem curses her children: *May her sons be born with extra nipples.*
It wishes her adult acne and a string of bad dates
followed by a string of bad marriages.

In fact, this poem is madder than I am. If it could
it would smite her with hair loss, eczema, tax audits, flat
tires, high cortisol levels, irritable bosses, irritable
bowel syndrome, halitosis, and irregular periods in white pants.

You might be disappointed in it—
yeah, it's got a mean streak. It can be a real asshole.
But you don't know its story. Maybe it grew up on the streets,
eating wilted lettuce from the dumpster behind Albertson's.

Maybe it was just passed up for a promotion
or its rent check bounced again
or its girlfriend left with the coffee maker and the CDs
but didn't take that goddamn Shih Tzu that pisses in the closet.

Or maybe its father just died
and it realized it will never be *half*
the poem he was.

Narcissist Revises Tidal Theory

*In questions of science, the authority of a thousand is not worth
the humble reasoning of a single individual.*
    —GALILEO

The October coast is not where one turns for comfort, yet
I'm drawn again to this abandoned stretch of rock and spray
where the thin-lipped horizon coughs a few rheumy clouds
and the wind grates its serrated edge against my neck.

Why? I find little pleasure in the sandpiper's mocking hops,
his parody of delight a foil to my despair, and the waves keep
repeating like a proverb, some once-useful warning now clichéd.

Galileo saw the tides as water sloshing in a pan, the earth's rotation
the cause, and admonished Kepler's folly for believing
the moon is the force which incites the waters to a tumult.

Both were fools. The tides are the metronome of my regret, powered
by perpetual hindsight. They set the currents spinning in a gyre
that collects the flotsam of my affairs—plastic spoons and condoms,

frozen dinner trays, snow globes, souvenirs, chewed pens, the woven
mesh of lawn chairs, a cooler lid, nurdles of exfoliating soap—and sends
it swirling in the Pacific to tangle in seaweed and clog seagulls' throats.

In return, the tides fork over a drying branch of coral, some worthless
shells, or sometimes a small shark, half-buried in a shallow sandbar,
whose flesh, when pressed, has unexpected give and whose discrete
cerulean eye glints like an omen I should know how to read.

Manic Depressive Wins Nobel Prize
for Getting It On

On those lush days when she feels so rich
>> the pocket of her heart can't hold all the rolls
> of hundreds bound with rubber bands,
>>> she is exuberant in her generosity.

She goes to coffee shops, parks, car washes to fall in love
> with strangers who look like her fifth-grade teachers
>> and '60s sit-com stars whose names she can't remember.

She loves, instantly and devoutly, the girl at the bus stop studying
>> Cliffs Notes, and the teenager foaming white drifts
> of skim milk for lattes, and the man at the dry cleaners
>>> who frowns as he gives her a claim stub for pants
>>> he will press and she will wrinkle again.

At the playground she watches the fathers peeling tangerines,
>> double-knotting shoelaces, fastening lids on cups of juice.
>> She wants to line them up and fuck them,
> little rewards for their patience.

She will do whatever each wants most, and she can tell
> what that is
> by one's laugh lines, another's bitten-down thumbnail.

And she'll take the two women arguing in the deli
>> over the last haunch of cracked pepper turkey

to the Wingate Inn, sit them on the edge of the double bed,

        slip off the pumps pinching their toes.

She'll kiss the arches of their feet, lick clavicle and ear lobe

        and moles beneath elbows, caress crow's feet

    and breasts equally, then rub a balm of wild fig

and love-in-idleness into their calves and thighs, until

        the world clenches and groans, softens and sighs.

Manic Depressive Visits Ocean with Lover
One Last Time

She finds it's not what she remembered, the sand coarser,
wind brittle, more insistent.
Even the current has changed directions, and she's lost
in the one-way streets of a city she was sure she knew.

She stumbles in the waves and twists beneath the green
water like the propeller of a rusted boat, shoulder, then thigh,
scraping fragments of seashells and the broken finger
of a starfish. As her lover jerks her to her feet,
their wrists click like the verbs of dolphins,
urgent and untranslatable.

At least she can practice her excuses over the roar and spray.
The wind lashes her words past his cupped ear,
past The Gypsy Inn and The Seafarer, paint peeling like sunburn,
past the balcony where her towel limply surrenders.

At dusk, she phones her husband from the hotel room.
There are things she wants to explain, like what's revealed
when the tide recedes, slipping like a blouse
off the sloped shoulder of the coast.

He only half listens. She knows he's watching TV, muted,
while she talks—maybe his favorite, the Travel Channel—
and she imagines his face flooded with light,

his skin tinged violet like the lips of a winter swimmer, gasping,

a swimmer struggling toward a distant, finer shore.

The Optimists' Birthday

Tomorrow they begin the year when everything they've wanted
will finally happen. They're already forgetting
the accumulated grievances. Regret rises from them
like shower steam. Falling asleep, they can hardly remember
the money that sifted through their fingers, the interviews
they blew, the trip to Cancun they didn't take,
hotel mints uneaten, waterfalls splashing in bodiless pools.

Gone, the disappointment of gonzo porn and parties
to which they weren't invited. Gone, too, the guilt of promises
that evaporated as they exhaled and the dental cleanings
they skipped, the unexposed film of their blank x-rays
a black hallway waiting for apparitions.

They're even forgetting the way death circled the edge of the room,
that chronic cough, the abscess that ate the fur off the dog's muzzle,
forgetting, too, the bird that hit the hood of the car and the pages
of the field guide in which they looked for and couldn't find
its grey head or the scarlet swipe above its bent neck.

They can hardly recall the fights and the score,
the inventory of what was thrown. And how long has it been
since they've thought of the week wasps appeared in their bed,
thrumming above the unmade sheets, or the worry of omens
as those veined wings vibrated on the pillows, glinting
like the thin crackling of frost on the windows?

II

Canticles, Maybe

Prayer to Saint Lawrence: For the Overcooked

For mothers with one culinary technique: well done,
　　　for the limp asparagus they lower back into the pot,
declaring, "Just another minute." For scrambled eggs hardening
　　　　　on breakfast buffets and NY strip three shades past medium,
　　　bring us ketchup and Tabasco sauce, hollandaise and ponzu.
Saint Lawrence, patron of chefs, drizzle au jus over every charred forkful.

For the highway in summer, smoking and blackened like a swordfish,
　　　for all that smolders in the drum of August—tattered grass, faces
leathered in fields, supermarket carnations shriveled graveside,
　　　bring us rain and hail, unexpected cold snaps, November's enamel of frost.

For the favorite uncles with cancer and the radiation that roasts
　　　their throats. Clear the fly ash of dead cells from the chimney flue
　　　　　of the esophagus and stitch new cords in the voice box.

Saint Lawrence, patron against fire, tortured on the gridiron,
　　　martyr who wisecracked, "Turn me over, this side's done,"
　　　　　lend us your high tolerance for pain, your dark humor.

For the searing dreams we wrench ourselves from at 2, at 3, at 4:30,
　　　soaked and shaking. Patron of laundry women and librarians,
　　　　　lay us down on the fresh sheets of our childhood beds
　　　　　　　　　　　and tell us stories
　　　of young Indian brides who self-immolate
　　　　　and wake swathed in aloe, cocooned in gauze,
freed, for a moment, of their husbands' hands

and the cat o'nine tails of their in-laws' tongues.

Patron of vintners, let us hold a cup to their lips,

knowing what they can't drink will be cool on their chins

and the new pink skin of their necks.

For the empty river bed in its reptilian stretch

toward the cracked horizon.

For the man trapped in the spiral shaft of a copper mine

who writes his wife, "When I sleep, I dream of ovens."

Patron of heat, patron of archives, send us wicking shirts and box fans,

ice melting in styrofoam and on foreheads.

If not these nor the Atlantic's gusts,

permit us the air-conditioned gasp of department store doors

or a rasp of air culled

by the paper fans of funeral homes.

Inheritance of Prayer and Luck

I hang the print above the master bedroom thermostat,
gilt flaking off the corners of the chipped frame,
paper yellowing unevenly, darkening like a tea stain
beneath the ornate, illustrated script—*Pray for us,*
O holy Mother of God, that we may be made worthy—

and I recall what I can of the hotel room she lived in:
rosary of pressed petals on the nightstand,
Christmas tree wound with garlands of glass beads
and plastic candy, glittering year round beside the TV,
and this print my mother held a moment on her lap
while labeling the artifacts of her grandmother's life:
Aunt Maureen, John's kids, garage sale, Goodwill.

As she sat on the edge of the pilled comforter
and read aloud, "Turn, then, most gracious Advocate,
thine eyes of mercy toward us," a housekeeper
crossing the patio with a cart of soaps and towels
pulled me from the pool I had wandered into
as if I could just stroll across the glinting water.

My Mother Demanded Gratitude

Bone-ache signaled growth,
height a sure thing.

Hiccups? The lungs' desire
to fulfill their contract with the body.

Stubbed toe, throbbing funny bone,
leg of pins and needles—

even a toothache, a blessing:
"If it hurts, it's not dead."

Any pain better than none, better
than the nerves' apathy.

And so she bubbled with laughter
when the car window closed

on my fingers or a camera swinging
from her chest clocked my forehead

as she picked me up, her joy boiling
over my pained but breathing body.

A Fable from the Palm-Leaf Manuscript

In third grade I made an alphabetical list of the children who had laughed at my eye patch and the one who stole the strawberries from my lunch and the one who rode horses and the ones who ignored me. I titled this list NERDS, the worst invective I knew how to spell. Then I threw it away, ashamed of my bitter accounting. Martin Harris (fourth, below Darby Handle, above Chris Stevenson) fished the paper from the trashcan and gave it to Mrs. Mason, who made me apologize, in writing, to each injured party. If this is a fable, what is the moral? What animal am I? What glass jar will fill with rain, raising what berry within my reach?

If I Raise My Daughter Catholic

Will she envy the nuns' stiff habits or steal
from my purse for the collection plate?

Will she sit with me on the edge of her bed
and admit sins she doesn't yet have
names for: masturbation, smolder of spite,
the rosary of envies she thumbs?

Will a boy strike the back of her legs
with a dogwood switch on the Immaculate Heart
of Mary playground, lighting an exquisite flare
like the sting of sweat bees? Will the nun
she runs to say, "That just means he likes you"?

Will she renounce her father's bacon-laced
meatloaf and curry-rubbed pork loin, eat only
raw foods and organic honey,
comb suspended in its amber reliquary?

When she takes Communion, will she hold
the Eucharist vertically in her mouth
to preserve it, thin edges pressed against
tongue and palate, like a photo album
lifted high in a flooded house?

Will she make a confessional of every space
she enters—doctor's office, cab of a pickup, blank
page, hollow of a lover's collar bone—
lips parted to issue an ecstasy of failings?

Late Period

During a week of waiting, I watched knots of school kids
trudging home each day, station wagons spitting grit and
dust into their faces, and thought I heard an echo of infants
behind drywall, muffled squalls I couldn't, didn't

want to follow. But it came, heavy, on my grandmother's chaise.
A cloth pressed to the stain bloomed red, then a paler red,
until the last white corner was stippled with pink sprays.
I expected to feel grateful: pardon granted, threat lifted.

But long after the stubbled velvet of the cushion had dried,
I smelled the mingled perfume of aunts, great-aunts, assorted
cousins, and my own brackish salt and iron. What relief could I
find when sleep kept returning me to a room with boarded

windows, light parted by slats like broken crib rails? On a worn
table, a curdled bottle and a doll, limbless and shorn.

Setting the Record Straight

Adam, I will tell them you were younger than first reported,
too small to reach the faucet or pack your own lunch.
I'll explain you were four and a half
and knelt in a chair in blue jeans, waiting for a snack.

Eve cried as she washed the apple, wept as she cored
the white meat, quartered the crisp heart,
and dropped the slick crescents in a sandwich bag.
She told you to sit on your bottom, not to rock the chair
or test your new head, your spine, or your ribs against the tile.
She told you she was taking you to the park.

This was true: she set you loose near the playground,
spinning across the grass like a dreidel. You held her
damp hands and danced through the leaves—How many
ways has this story been told?—as the quarter moons
in her apron pocket darkened and dusk deepened
under branches the color of eggplant, your wind-burnt cheeks
as brilliant as a Red Delicious, your hunger coiling.

Passages from the Travel Diary of Noah's Wife

APRIL 9

Was it a sin to feel smug standing on the deck beside him,
arms folded, listing as the waters rose, closing over
the tops of thatched huts, and the boat,
sealed in pitch, lifted up like an awkward pelican?

Now I haven't slept in days and I no longer worry
about the rain but instead the mold, persistent,
inching over flanks and hooves.
Each night we lie side by side in the hay without touching
(Yahweh save us, there is hay everywhere)
as the darkness moves, takes breath in pairs.

APRIL 16

Noah has withdrawn, as the tide once pulled from the shore.
He talks only of the basil and dill drowning in the garden,
the rosemary and thyme tangling like seaweed.

What will be left when the water recedes?
Crustaceans sucking on the bark of cedars and pines?
Will the hills have washed into the valleys,
leaving the land as gently sloped as a collar bone?

APRIL 25

Each day we shovel dung and feathers overboard.
We drink rain from oak barrels.
Our store of grain is clumped and mealy,
but the tubers seem inspired by the humidity.
The sweet potato and the turnip are trying to take root,
clawing into the dirt between the planks.

We do not discuss those left behind,
aardvark, possum, child—
all whose lungs had once been sleek fish
rippling behind the coral of ribs.

MAY 8

This morning, a silence.
The llamas and the penguins froze,
and in the rafters, the crests of the black palms lifted.
Noah swung the swollen hatch open
to find the sun had returned like a letter
and we squinted to read it,
inching forward stiffly across
the warped planks of the bow.

MAY 15

After lunch the cap of a hill appeared,
steaming like a loaf of bread,
and as I write I can't help but remember
my sister's sweaty thighs
and the mossy head of her son
crowning between them.

Prayer to Saint Joseph: For the Restless

Saint Joseph, stepfather of Christ, patron of moving, patron
against doubt, lead us not to Seattle or LA or SoHo
when unease thickens like lime calcifying

in the porcelain basins of our chests. Lead us not
into the temptation of sublets or studio walk-ups
that get good afternoon light in our imagination.

Patron of real estate agents, deafen our ears to the call
of subdivisions with shorter commutes and condos
our lovers will swoon to enter, with brass-fixtured bathrooms

they will never lock themselves in to weep.
Patron of immigrants, let us think not on the president
of Kazakhstan, who moved his capital to a frozen steppe

and there built an aquarium and a glass pyramid
of dark-loamed, path-stitched gardens. Let us not be quick
to split when we bankrupt our small countries. O patron

of travelers and wheelwrights, when the wallpaper ripples
in the humidity of our malaise and the carpet is worn
to a sheen by our pacing, stop us before we put our houses

on the market and bury your statue in the backyard
for luck. You who know the summons
of the journey, remind us of the friend who left town

in the middle of the week, abandoning
a mattress and a lease, and whom we later learned
stepped off a bridge, holding hands with his loneliness.

Still our hands as we pack. Remind us the roughest fabric
of the self will end up folded like a sweater
in the suitcase, pilled and raveled and transcendent.

Plea of the Penitent

Forgive us our sins, mostly the result of a deficit of attention.
  Options tower on pallets and we wander the aisles, dazed
warehouse shoppers recklessly grabbing gallon tubs of Thousand Island
  when what we need are paper towels and bleach.

We want to try to do better, to try again, to try not to
  one more time and this time really not—not down
another World's Best Dad mug of Maker's Mark,
  not smoke another last cigarette—not even a menthol
ultra light, not even on the porch, away from the baby—

not cheat at cards or on our husbands, not play another hand,
  bet another next month's paycheck or let another palm
coast our thighs, drawing a straight flush from skin
  that thrills even as foreboding floods the cellars of our heart.

We're the best-selling authors of grave mistakes.
  Our advance is regret, six figures, but never enough
for a down payment on restraint. We're sincere as hell, though,
  when we apologize, pleading into the disconnect tone
or mouthing the rosary after confession, even as we plot
  what we can write next on this blank slate.

Give us this day our daily second chance. Let us atone like the Hindus
  who lift curses by marrying strays draped in yellow saris
and garlands of jasmines and orchids. Take us to the pound

in Leon County, to the gravel runs in the back.

Show us the arthritic husky or tumored retriever, the one shivering

with anticipation for the long car ride home.

A Proverb from the Palm-Leaf Manuscript

This is what I will tell you: my best friend in middle school pulled clumps of her hair out while her uncle raped her, and then she pulled her hair out during breakfast, homeroom, algebra, geography, and world lit, littering blond strands across stubbled carpet and linoleum and right down the halls of Saint Joseph's long-term ward until the floor glittered like Indian cloth shot through with gold thread.

Are you as surprised as I was to hear she still calls him on Sundays from a payphone?

For two decades I worried this knot. Then the elders offered a proverb: For the traveler with both legs broken, frostbite proves a balm, stinging nettle a caress, the strike of the asp a sweetness. They know the god of memory waits by the river, chewing a bitter root and honing his scythe on a coarse-grained stone.

The Thing You Might Not Understand

when I tell you the man whose children I babysat in college
cornered me on the deck after the party and copped a feel

is how his eyes looked drunk, glassy but sad,
and how his smile tilted apologetically but his body

was straight and formal, as if we were dignitaries shaking hands,
or how he held my breast as gently as I cupped his daughter's head

the first time I washed her in the kitchen sink,
rubbing the cradle cap from her hair with baby oil,

palming warm water over her head, pale silk strands
swirling like fine crackling in the glaze of old porcelain,

the veins of her eyelids a faint calligraphy on vellum,
the extant manuscript that would reveal, if we could translate it,

a treatise on forgiveness, or canticles, maybe,
a tune we sometimes hum, unaware, under our breath

as we walk to the mailbox, or fill a birdfeeder with seed,
or lower a man's hand and lead him back into his house.

Assurances to a Friend in Her Third Trimester

All you have to do is relearn how to pray,
remember how the knees bend (think *compass*,
accordion, *hinge*), how the palms align and press
like tectonic plates. Then the rising diphthongs
of a new language will two-step on your tongue.

All you have to do is reinvent breathing,
design a system of copper pipes, elbow joints,
and welded branches with hidden bellows
and a fail-safe switch. Calibrate the valves
for fluctuations caused by weeping.
Now replicate it, one-tenth the size.

Then all that's left is to fossilize into calcite
and hold your arms as steady as Saint Kevin,
in whose prayer-raised palm a blackbird wove
a nest of moss and roots and laid an egg.
Think of him kneeling there beneath a window.
The first tap of the egg tooth.
See, you already know what to do.

Amulet

The preschoolers are playing a new
                kind of dodge ball a fifth-grader

taught them. When hit, they retract an arm
                into their shirts, then pull up one leg,

then the other, until a boy becomes
                an ampersand typed on the grass.

Soon the lawn is studded
                with these seed pearls of boys.

The smallest, first out again, forges through
                the rock garden, shirt above his belly.

He sits beside me on the garden wall
                and asks, "Will you hold my babies?"

unrolling the warm fabric to expose
                three pebbles, flecked amber and gold.

I rub them between my palms like dice
                and blow into my cupped hands.

Tucked inside my sock, they bite my ankle
                with the first exciting heat of luck.

Middle Class Love Song

When some know-it-all on public radio insists income
        is more hereditary than height or weight, and some other

dour economist agrees we're on the fast track back to serfdom,
        we shrug, so yeah, maybe everybody's broke, but not too broke

to catch a matinee at Miracle 8 or grab a venti from Starbucks,
        and ok, our rental looks kinda trashy, the jasmine vine dying

on the chain-link in a gothic brown tangle—poisoned, we think,
        by our duplex neighbor's latest crazy ex—but we're rich in

monkey grass, which spreads so wildly that the neighbor's kid
        just mows it down in a verdant stubble, and we may not have

tidy box hedges or a golf cart to tootle around the block in,
        like the doctor in the McMansion next door, his yellow

labs loping in the wake of his cigar smoke, but we also don't
        have his patients suing us for urethral surgery mishaps,

and we can hear the jazz from the Bose speakers of his gazebo on dusky
        Sunday evenings, and we dance on our front stoop,

just hugging really, a long swaying hug, and at least we have
        this cement stoop, right?, and this fenced yard our dog patrols

with full-hearted devotion, as if she's guarding the Taj Mahal,

    and Coltrane on a humid breeze and our hug dances and our glossy

textbook of crazy exes and the medieval tapestry of our jealousies—

    not to mention the pleasure of knowing our children

and our children's children will have ever-increasing latte options

    and even richer neighbors and even crazier, more creative exes.

Conception Psalm

When the seed pearls tremble
      and swell, coiled in the satin
purse of the ovary, when the clasp breaks
      and one falls,
then unwind the body

      like a bolt of cloth,
trace a pattern on the fine weave.
      Raise the tongue, so long sealed
in the envelope
      of the mouth. Apologize
to the clavicle for its neglect,

beg forgiveness of the lonesome
      shoulder blades.
    Moon-rinse the breasts, pebble
the areolas. Spread the lips

      and the lips. Find the clit hidden
in its curio case, dust it
    with tongue and thumb.

Find the balls lolling in the shade.
      Let the mouth sing them awake!

The mouth will know
            it is time.
        The lungs will know and tell
the breath, the sternum will tell the ribs,
        the ribs,
                the arching length of spine.

No doubt the arching cock
            also will know. Let the cock say
what it's been thinking,
        and may the one glistening
                    seed pearl hear

those shouted words of blessing.

III

Rustle of Offerings

When We Have Lived
for Thirty Years in One Town

We drive home from dinner, usually
a little too full, sometimes satisfied
with our lives, sometimes not,
the little vents in the dashboard offering
their cold blessing, the murmur of air
intoning *You can change your lot*, or sometimes
Comfort is possible, and it seems for a moment
to come to us like a present
we ordered for ourselves online.

As we near the interstate, you ask,
"Which way? East or west?"
and I remind you
that by the strange virtue of our geography
home is always to the east.

Think of the Orient, *orientation*, of curled maps,
those stories of ancient travelers, their camels
snorting and spitting softly
over moon-rinsed drifts, camels swaying
under the weight of men drowsing
on flea-knitted blankets, flasks of oil
and leather pouches of coins, turmeric,
and cardamom belted to their hips, men cloaked
in the certainty of where they're headed
and what they'll find there.

How Do You Say

Reaching for the phone, I step on the dog's tail,
and she nuzzles my ankle in apologetic
reverence, her perpetual state.

Another friend is calling
for congratulations.
                        Another engagement!

Everyone I know is thinking of falling in love
or falling out of love, either way with both feet on the edge
like the concrete lip of the deep end

and shimmering before them, the cold, drowning water
of adoration or the cold, drowning water of loneliness,
and everyone is referring to the languages of love,

though no one seems to have read the book,
just flipped through the table of contents
at Wal-Mart, but it's enough to know

not all of the languages of love are actual languages,
not French, as you might expect, *mon amour*,
or Italian, *Ti amo, vita mia*, but the language of sweeping

the garage without being asked or necking at the movies
or scooping out the litter box,
so the broom's metronome counts the beat of love

and tongues trace the calligraphy of love
on the cartouche of collarbone, and for my friend
with the pregnant wife, even the kitty litter

spells out love with its alphabet of odors
as he scoops clumps of piss, hissing over his shoulder
at the cats who lattice the shower curtain

and burrow in the mattress, because for cats
the language of love and the language of possession
are lyrics to the same aria, while dogs, those Mozarts,

hum just one uncomplicated bar over and over,
yet we hear the swelling of a symphony.

An Increase in the Cost of Living

The ocean of my love for you is threatening to flood
the B-list celebrities and low carb diets of your California,
and it's only going to get worse. The Health Department

placed Leghorn chickens across the county to track West Nile.
Mosquitoes, preferring dark meat, nestle through feathers
to suck the thighs. When you have been strategically placed

for such a purpose, you are called a sentinel chicken. August Ursin,
government worker, swings each chicken by the legs before
drawing blood. Stunned, the chickens submit.

You never asked that much of me, but lover, I broke my promise
not to shop at Wal-Mart. Do you know how much produce
costs these days? Are bananas fifty cents a pound? A dollar?

How can we communicate when you always assume
my questions are rhetorical? At Wal-Mart, a man blocking
the doors with a Budweiser truck was arguing with a cop,

cop insisting Shelley Winters had to be the worst actress who
ever lived, Budweiser sputtering, "Have you not seen
The Money Pit?" I should have told Budweiser he was thinking

of Shelley Long but the cop was already writing him a ticket.
Lover, whose good name will we defend, mistaken but intense,
some humid night? The lab results are in. We're at risk

for hypertension, kidney failure, anemia, and chronic
disillusionment. Enjoy that banana, love. It's a Cavendish,
the genetic twin of every other grocery-store banana, perfect

and seedless but not as sweet as the last variety, those Big Mike
bananas wiped out by Panama disease. You can stay the night but
you should know, my grandma sends prayer cards, unsigned checks

for ten bucks, and once a fake penny the size of my palm.
I put them under my pillow. Lot of good it will do, sure,
but without that rustle of offerings, I would lie awake, stunned.

A Physics Lesson from the Palm-Leaf Manuscript

When I heard two friends I hadn't seen in years had left their spouses and moved in together, I felt the slap of betrayal. The elders chided me and pointed to the river: "Impact depends on velocity and distance."

Water, we know, can caress the skin like a washed-to-softness cotton shirt or the memory of our mothers brushing our hair back off our foreheads. From here, at the railing of the bridge, the river is a wide ribbon of dimes, tumbling and glinting with the lure of easy money. But if we jumped, the crests wouldn't part to admit us; they'd stiffen hard as the sidewalk.

Who can describe that shattering? Only the suicides, returned as bristling tabbies or quick-to-ball-up armadillos. But how many lives do they have to work through before they earn back the language to tell us?

Why You Shouldn't Find
an Old Childhood Friend Online

Because your mother's praise of her, *such a sweet child,*
how I wish I had such a generous girl, is a scab you pick
with the chewed fingernail of memory.

Because she's started a quilting circle or a church in her basement,
and she'll want you to join it.

Because she dropped out of college and works in a mall kiosk
plucking eyebrows and applying acrylic tips,
or she finished her PhD in two years and won a Fulbright.

Because her favorite shows are *Judge Judy* and *The Pet Psychic,*
and she plays internet canasta on nights she's not singing
in amateur Baroque operas performed in church basements.

Because she's written a bad novel, a story of heroin
and redemption, and she'll ask you to read it.

Because she won't remember the color of the stray cat
you buried together in the shade of the birdbath.

Because from time to time you still think of her older brother
belting out Journey and Air Supply in his bedroom, and how sure you felt
he was adjectives you didn't understand: *sexy, fine, hung.*

Because she'll tell you he had a stroke in his dormitory shower,
died with his ear pressed to the tile,
skin sloughing as he lay there for hours,

and you'll press your own ear to the cold shower wall to listen
for what words he might have heard in the endless echo of water.

Stopping for the Night at Motel 6

I push aside the hotel pillow on which
a woman's hair might have dried
and lie stiffly, as she might have,
one of two bodies separated, a couple
with their backs turned. My heart groans
against the rusted springs of my ribs.

In the storm yesterday I watched a gull, exhausted,
trying to land on the ledge of a parking deck,
pushed back again and again by the gale.

My husband lifts my wet hair off my neck.
"Did I ever tell you about my cousin?
He was murdered during a riot in Detroit.
Beaten to death behind a dumpster.
My aunt was interviewed on the morning news."

I stop crying to consider his story,
this new attempt at comfort,
an invitation to share a used-up sadness.

I run my arm in the dip of the mattress
where others must have relented.
My body softens, we slip
into the impression of past lovers.

Property Manager's Word of Warning

If you must walk the dogs alone after midnight,
  clutch your keys with their teeth jutting
    from your fist, a make-shift weapon,
as advised in the apartment newsletter
beneath the incident report and the legal disclaimer,
  gentle reminder that no one
(especially management) can be responsible
  for your personal safety,

or the safety of the black hatchback, windshield shattered,
or the woman from 3-B, mugged,
  her 18-hour lipstick, bus pass, and tampons
    discarded behind the tennis courts,
and certainly not the children unattended,
  plucked from the playground, one sister caught
half-way down the slide, the other lifted
  from the swing in mid-air, her hair floating
  behind her like a ransom note.

Be aware of your surroundings. Have your weapon ready.
  Your sneakers grinding the gravel path
    sound like a zipper coming down,
as the dogs drag you toward the woods,
  their leashes strangling your palm.
They bark at the pear trees, the wisteria,

at something you cannot see: discarded pipes, choked vines,
trees with their branches clenched
like men with cocked fists.

Language Lessons

I point to the geometry of light
where the curtains refuse to meet,
the south and south of two magnets.

You wrestle the stubborn fabric back,
summoning the orange interrogation
of the streetlamp, light unspooling
questions across the quilt, the dresser,
the half-open drawer of knotted scarves.

Voices rise from the parking lot,
two women arguing in Spanish,
words like the clatter
of boxes falling down a flight of stairs.

Last night you taught me the words for arm and leg.
Tonight I want *mouth, bed, kiss,*
and again the word for the back of the hand.

Cock, an Etymology

When I slip my arms around your sides as you lean
at the sink washing dishes and plough my cold hands
down the front of your jeans to feel the heat rising
from its hidden nest, I'm thinking of the man
on the drugstore sidewalk who touched my arm

and pointed to a rooster on a leash strutting across
the parking lot. We marveled at his knobby comb,
his copper and feldspar feathers, and that long neck
thrusting forward, beak stabbing indifferently
at truck tire, discarded paper cup, shopping cart, air.

Yet when I approached, the owner offered, "Go on,
he's harmless." I sunk my fingers into the feathers
to stroke the spindly neck, at once delicate but firm,
like bundled reeds, and then hurried home to you,
in love again with nomenclature and your anatomy.

Postcard from the Sapelo River

It's true, the weather is beautiful, cool enough
    for a sleeve, and almost cloudless,
        the wind rocking the warm planks
of the dock where I play backgammon
    with my host and eat sandwiches
        in crustless triangles. After lunch I read
on the porch, an afghan smoothed
    over my knees and a highball perched
        on a stack of Harlequins beside the loveseat.
The days pass easily, as you said they would.

But if you were here, my dearest, my most
    comfortable of loves, I could belch, scratch my armpits,
        and sit with my legs splayed.
I could nap in ripped underwear, drool on the arm
    of the couch. And when I grew bored, I would bat
        the newspaper from your hands and tease,
The Spanish moss in the oaks looks like pubic hair.

We'd shower together in water pumped
    from the river, stand drying before a box fan,
        then lie down smelling like coins, counting
our wealth, lie damp with the sheen
    of the river at midday gleaming
        on my breasts, your thighs, our laced arms

beneath the pleated rice-paper curtains

    held up with clothespins, the window open

        to the banks, to their cordgrass and mussels

and the steady current that pulses between them.

Useless Valediction Forbidding Mourning

"It's just a week," you repeat. "Just seven days."
        Tell that to the heart, gripping its abacus,
        worrying the bead of each hour.

You claim, "Scientists have clocked neutrinos moving faster
than the speed of light, and that's how fast I'll come home."
        Tell that to the veins, dragging dread
        through the body like a felled tree.

"We'll talk four times a day at least," you coax.
        Tell that to the tongue, fumbling through
        its phrase book of conversational heartbreak.

"When you wake up on Sunday, I'll be home," you promise.
        Tell that to the molars, those hopeless insomniacs,
        grinding through the graveyard shift.

"It's only two hours east," you remind me.
        Tell that to the heart. The heart has no use
        for cartography, chicken scratch of the lost.

"Remember that poem?" you ask. "You're the fixed foot
of the compass."
        Tell that to the cortex, revving the engine
        of the limbic system, flooding the carburetor with panic.

"We're gold beat to airy thinness," you wheedle.

Oh, but the heart isn't fooled

by the gorgeous lies of poems.

Trying Not to Cry Before Dinner

The backyard is frozen
in patches of mud and silver grass,
a garden of broken TVs and rotting lumber.
You promised to build a tool shed
but the planks have sunk into the mud.
The kitchen is filling with steam.
Corn silk clogs the disposal, the stems
of mushrooms and broccoli float in the sink.
I count TVs through the window
as a thin fog rises from the piles
of parts of things that are no longer useful.
The fog climbs the clapboards,
tendrils creep up the window, a ghost of ivy.
You test the air like tasting soup,
using a low word like a spoon.
You clear your throat,
say you have felt me turn cold
like a voice after a long pause on the telephone.
You turn the corn with a fork
as the water boils.
You say to the corn, "Don't cry, don't cry."
A sudden, invisible rain begins pushing the fog back,
pushing the fog down off the window,
flooding the tires and the ditches you dug
for tulip bulbs and golf.
I tell you I am going to sit on the porch.
I hold very still in the porch swing and wait

for you to come outside and light a cigarette,
small comfort against the rain
and the temperature dropping
like a hand after a wave.

A Definition from the Palm-Leaf Manuscript

When I record my weekend on the scroll of eventual reckoning—*Saturday, 2 a.m., drove alone down I-10, screaming at deaf mile markers; Sunday afternoon, curled on the sofa, weeping inconsolably*—the elders, deciphering my scrawl, echo "Inconsolably?"

They note the word means consolation was offered, an arm cloaking my shoulders, a hand drawing my head to a chest, behind which a heartbeat played its étude of empathy, and I could have listened, I could have breathed in time.

Why I Did Not Proceed with the Divorce

Because I've heard of a man who lay
his left leg across train tracks
to show his sons
how to celebrate loss.

And when I was thirteen, my father
swabbed blood on our front door
after he moved out,

maybe to protect us, but more likely
to declare, *Behold:*
the threshold of my last life,
or however you say that in Latin.

But mostly, because I slept in the guestroom
for six months
and you tapped on the door
each night, offering a glass of water.

Prayer to Saint John the Dwarf:
Against Giving Up

When we take our sad accounting,
trumpet lying mute, brass throat closed
with thick closet air, guitar amplifier
turned end table, balsa torso of a model
airplane, unpainted, a pale, wingless bird,

when we tally the abandoned
attempts, the cemented bristles
of unwashed paint brushes, half-knitted
scarves, pot-holder length, *Moby Dick*
dog eared at page forty-eight, blank
job applications, a marriage ditched
like a Chevy Nova in a Kmart parking lot,

we'll turn to you, Saint John, you who trekked
twelve miles each day through
the Nitrian Desert to water a planted walking
stick, some stripped limb of sycamore,
until it took root in the third year,
sucked deeply of the tended soil,
and bore a miracle of plums which, when bit,
dripped cold nectar into your brothers' beards.

Grant us your patience, Saint John, your faith,
your great stupidity or perseverance—
whichever blessed quality will lead us

to pick up the brush, the pen, the phone,
to lift the trumpet to our lips and sound
an exalted, off-key F.

A Theory on the Missing Leaves
of the Palm-Leaf Manuscript

Each sheaf constructed with such effort.
Broad-shouldered eldest daughters shimmying
trunks of talipot palms to cull the wide, mature leaves,
the bark a beard on their thighs.
Splitting each leaf down the midrib, boiling the strips
in brine and turmeric.
Then the drying, smoking, sanding with nubs of pumice—
all before the work of the scribe: etching letters
with an iron stylus (hook and crimp of fingers,
crick of back and knucklebone), rubbing lampblack
into the words, wiping the extra soot
with a folded scarf.

           Yet, see, this stitch is loose
where a leaf was removed, and fibers cling to the thread
like a patch of a vanished girl's dress caught
on a bramble. What was recorded that couldn't be born?

The elders won't say
           but remind me some words
throb on the page like nerves when flesh is flayed to bone.

Never Trust a Poem that Begins with a Dream

unless it's a love poem or the dream is the one you keep having
      where you leave a raucous party—the kind of party you're never
invited to—and sit on the balcony, just starting to tear up but not yet

      crying. Most nights the balcony is the second-story walkway of a motel
and the party is in full swing in the room behind you—The White Stripes
          vibrating the stucco and someone's cigarette, you imagine, burning

holes in the bedspread. A man always follows you out, and as you're trying
to remember who said "Loneliness is the first thing which God's eye named,
          not good," he puts his arm around you and whispers

something you never remember when you wake up, like the scene
      in an arty film where you don't get to hear the mumbled last words.
Some nights he's the boy you had a crush on in eighth grade

who did, in fact, put his arm across your shoulders in the cafeteria, sparks
      cascading down your back, under the Peter Pan-collared Catholic school girl
      blouse you wore un-ironically, being a Catholic school girl.

      Other nights he's the biology teacher who told oral sex jokes but
let you take a C minus instead of dissecting the frog and fetal pig, even let
      you leave the room during the dissecting, to escape that sharp odor

and soft, snipping sounds. But in the dream you aren't thinking
      how amazing it is you even graduated, given how much
      you refused to do and how often you skipped class to get stoned

behind the library, and you're not realizing gratefully how many concessions
         pity won you. Instead you're noticing how his breath on your ear
lets you feel those delicate folds of skin you rarely think of,

         the way wind moving through grass lets you see the separate blades.
But then you start to notice, too, the same adult-touching-a-child-
         in-an-overly-intimate-but-not-quite-inappropriate-way ickiness you felt

         when a family friend stroked your silky seven-year-old head and promised,
         "I'll take you away with me. You'll be my child bride." And then
you remember—in the dream—the joke the biology teacher told that ended

         "sucking the chrome off a trailer hitch." Other nights he's the dentist who
tightened your braces or the guy in college who sang you "Purple Rain"
         while he played a keyboard, whom you felt sorry for and kissed.

Or the Pakistani dry cleaner who proposed, pledging robust sons
         and starched slacks. But on the best nights, when you've fallen
         asleep with the right mix of herbal tea and *Law and Order* reruns,

he's your husband,
         the one you had or have or will have, your husband's arm
the right weight and length to drape your shoulders as you brood
         "which God's eye named, not good . . . which God's eye named,
not good" and his voice is warm in your hair, answering,
                  "It was Milton. Ready to go home?"

Acknowledgments

I would like to thank the editors and staff at the following journals where these poems first appeared, sometimes in slightly different versions or with earlier titles.

32 Poems: "Amulet," "Trying Not to Cry Before Dinner"

AGNI Online: "Prayer to Saint Joseph: For the Restless"

Bellingham Review: "Assurances to a Friend in Her Third Trimester," "Veneration of the Anxious"

Beloit Poetry Journal: "Passages from the Travel Diary of Noah's Wife"

Best New Poets 2008: "The Thing You Might Not Understand"

The Comstock Review: "Cock, an Etymology," "Property Manager's Word of Warning"

Crab Orchard Review: "When We Have Lived for Thirty Years in One Town"

Juked: "A Fable from the Palm-Leaf Manuscript"

The Ledge: "The Failed Revolutionaries Apologize to Their Foreign Sponsors"

Meridian: "Why the Lepidopterist Lives Alone," "Why You Shouldn't Find an Old Childhood Friend Online"

New Letters: "The Fortune Teller Knows She'll Never Marry," "Manic Depressive Wins Nobel Prize for Getting It On," "A Myth from the Palm-Leaf Manuscript," "The Optimists' Birthday," "A Vindictive Son of a Bitch of a Poem"

Nimrod: "How Do You Say," "Middle Class Love Song," "A Proverb from the Palm-Leaf Manuscript," "An Unfinished Fairytale from the Palm-Leaf Manuscript"

Painted Bride Quarterly: "Postcard from the Sapelo River"

Ploughshares: "Narcissist Revises Tidal Theory," "Never Trust a Poem that Begins with a Dream"

Reed Magazine: "My Mother Demanded Gratitude"

River City: "Setting the Record Straight"

River Styx: "Plea of the Penitent"

The Southeast Review: "If I Raise My Daughter Catholic"

The Southern Review: "Prayer to Saint Lawrence: For the Overcooked"

Sow's Ear: "Conception Psalm"

TriQuarterly: "The Compulsive Liar Apologizes to Her Therapist for Certain Fabrications and Omissions"

Whiskey Island: "Language Lessons"

"Trying Not to Cry Before Dinner" appears in *Old Flame: From the First 10 Years of 32 Poems Magazine* (WordFarm, 2013).

I am endlessly grateful to the teachers, friends, and family who have provided encouragement and insight, especially David Kirby, Barbara Hamby, Anne Coldiron, Julianna Baggott, Kim Addonizio, David Bottoms, Beth Gylys, Leon Stokesbury, Rebecca Lehmann, Jen McClanaghan, Laci Mattison, Sandra Simonds, Brandi George, Michael Barach, Vincent Guerra, Jen Schomburg Kanke, Paula Walborsky, Kent Putnam, Katie Chaple, Holly Selph, Josie and Fred Nevill, Andrew Pallos, and Royal Yu. Thank you, Dana Curtis and Sarah Kennedy, for bringing this book into existence.

Titles from Elixir Press